Science
Success

Terry Jenn

4

OXFORD
UNIVERSITY PRESS

Acknowledgements

The author and publisher would like to thank the following for help in the preparation of this book:
Jeremy and Lourdes Cottam; Donal and Jenny McCarthy, and Neville McGeorge.

Photographic credits

Bo'sun /R D Battersby pp 8 (bottom), 16, 27, 34 (top, bottom left, centre, bottom right), 39, 40, 42 (left, right), 43, 44 (top, bottom), 46, 47 (top, centre, bottom), 48 (top), 57, 60 (left) /Claire Williams p 56 (top); courtesy of British Airways p 36 (top); Eye Ubiquitous /Peter Blake p 32 /David Cohen p 18 /John Dakers pp 17, 58 (top) /S Miller p 51 /L R Miles p 54 (bottom) /H Rogers p 58 (bottom) /Paul Seheult p 59 /Stephen Rafferty p 30; James Davis Worldwide p 60 (right); Terry Jennings pp 6 (bottom), 7, 10 (left, right), 11, 48 (bottom), 49; Science Photo Library /Dr Jeremy Burgess p 54 (top) /A B Dowsett p 52 /Simon Fraser p 53 /Adrienne Hart-Davis p 56 (bottom) /John Mead p 31 (top) /Philippe Plailly p 31 (bottom) /NASA p 33; Skyscan/GR Photography p 36 (bottom); Sylvia Cordaiy Photo Library /Chris Parker p 50 (top) /Jonathan Smith p 50 (bottom); Telegraph Colour Library p 55 /Messersmidt p 28 /Tom Paiva p 41.

OXFORD
UNIVERSITY PRESS·

Great Clarendon Street, Oxford OX2 6DP

Oxford University Press is a department of the University of Oxford. It furthers the University's objective of excellence in research, scholarship, and education by publishing worldwide in

Oxford New York

Auckland Bangkok Buenos Aires Cape Town Chennai
Dar es Salaam Delhi Hong Kong Istanbul Karachi Kolkata
Kuala Lumpur Madrid Melbourne Mexico City Mumbai Nairobi
São Paulo Shanghai Taipei Tokyo Toronto

Oxford is a registered trade mark of Oxford University Press in the UK and in certain other countries

© Terry Jennings 2000

The moral rights of the author have been asserted

Database right Oxford University Press (maker)

First published 2000

20 19 18 17 16 15 14 13 12 11 10 9

ISBN 0 19 918341 4

Editorial, design and picture research by Lodestone Publishing Limited, Uckfield, East Sussex

Illustrations by Bob Chapman, Roger Gorringe, Nick Hawken, Michael Ogden, Julie Tolliday, and Dawn Brend

Science consultant: Dr Julian Rowe

Language consultant: Ann Mepham

Cover design: Oxford Designers and Illustrators

Printed in Spain by Gráficas Estella

Contents

(and suggested order of teaching)

Feeding relationships

All living things need food to grow and stay alive. Plants make their own food using water, carbon dioxide and light. This process is called **photosynthesis**. Inside a plant's leaves is a green substance called **chlorophyll**. Chlorophyll traps the energy from sunlight. The plant then uses this energy to turn carbon dioxide and water into the plant's food.

Leaves are usually large and flat so that they can absorb as much light as possible. The veins in the leaves carry water and mineral salts from the roots into the leaves. They also carry the food away to other parts of the plant.

Producers and consumers

Because plants are the only living things that can make their own food they are called **producers**. An animal that feeds on plants is called a primary **consumer**. An animal that feeds on a primary consumer is called a secondary consumer. It is also called a **predator**, and the animal it feeds on is called the **prey**. **Herbivores**, such as sheep, deer and giraffes, are primary consumers. Predators, such as lions and eagles, are secondary consumers. The relationship between the animals and plants in a habitat can be shown by **food chains**.

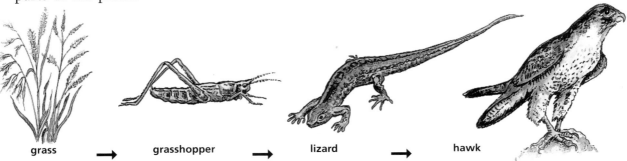

grass → grasshopper → lizard → hawk

A food chain with four links.

Food chains

A food chain shows the way energy flows through a **habitat**. Food chains usually start with a producer, a green plant, because that is where energy (from the sun) enters the food chain. The producer is then eaten by a primary consumer (an animal) which may then be eaten by a secondary consumer (another animal).

Food chains are usually made of three or four **organisms**.

lettuce →	rabbit →	fox
producer →	primary consumer →	secondary consumer
	herbivore	carnivore
	prey	predator

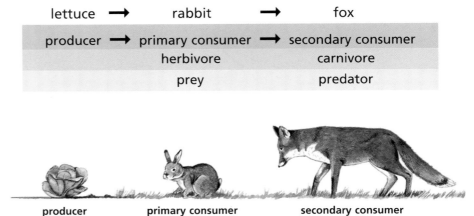

producer   primary consumer   secondary consumer

A simple food chain with three links.

There will be several food chains in any habitat. This is because there may be many kinds of animals that feed on the same plants and there are many predators that feed on the same kinds of prey. Food chains from the same habitat are sometimes linked together as a **food web**.

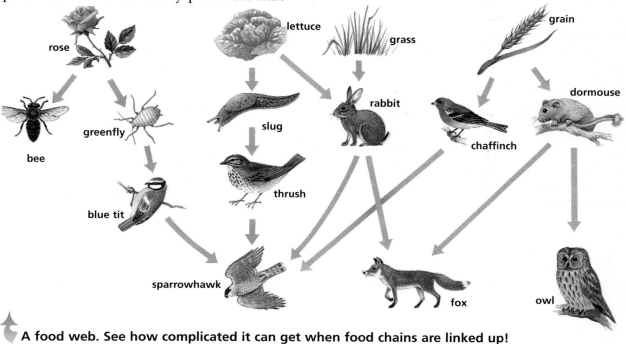

🦅 A food web. See how complicated it can get when food chains are linked up!

Questions

1 a What is the largest herbivore you can think of?
  b What is the largest secondary consumer (or predator) you can think of?
  c Secondary consumers (or predators) are sometimes smaller than the herbivores they feed on. Think of some examples, then discuss with a friend why this happens.

2 a Divide the living things in the box into producers, primary consumers, and secondary consumers.
  b Make and draw food chains using the plants and animals from the box.

```
grass   sheep   fox    lion   cabbage
eagle   wood mouse   lettuce   greenfly
antelope   ladybird   oak tree   thrush
      tawny owl   caterpillar   cod
   seaweed   limpet   shark   slug
```

3 What do you think would happen to all the plants and herbivores in an area if all the secondary consumers (or predators) were killed?

4 a Draw a food chain of which you are a part.
  b What do you think would happen if the plants at the beginning of a food chain were sprayed with a poisonous chemical?

River wildlife

rain or snow

fast-flowing tributaries

waterfall

meanders

salt marsh

estuary

sea

Most rivers begin, or have their source, in hills or mountains. They then flow down to the sea. Many plants and animals live in or near rivers. The different stages in the river also have different kinds of wildlife suited to living there.

The upper reaches

The water in the upper parts of a river is cold, clear and fast-flowing. Few plants can survive there because they are washed off the rocks. Apart from some water insects that live under the rocks, few animals live in this part of the river, although some fish, including trout and bullhead, may swim there against the strong current.

Water shrimps, crayfish and insects live further down the river. They provide food for fish, including salmon and minnows. The fish, in turn, are food for birds, such as kingfishers and herons, as well as for mammals like the otter.

Lowland river

The winding lowland parts of a river contain muddy, slightly warmer water, which flows more slowly. Plants grow in the bed of the river and at its edges. Dragonflies and many other species of insect live there, as do fish such as pike, perch, roach and bream. Swans and moorhens may feed on the water plants and animals, while water voles live in the river banks and feed on the plants growing there.

The stages in the life of a river.

The avocet has long legs for wading in the shallow waters of an estuary. It uses its curved beak to sift tiny animals from the muddy water.

Estuaries

Where a river meets the sea, its valley may widen out into a stretch of open water called an estuary. In sheltered estuaries some of the mud and sand carried by the river builds up to form salt marshes, which quickly become home to plants, and animals such as the shore crab. Some fish, such as flounders, can withstand the mixture of fresh and salt water. Huge flocks of ducks, geese and waders feed on the thousands of small animals – shellfish, worms and shrimps – that live in the mud. These small animals feed on the decaying plant and animal matter there.

Questions

1 a How is a fish suited to living in water?
  b Use resource material (books, CD-ROMs and the Internet) to find out as much as you can about the fish found in rivers in different parts of the world.

2 To help them to survive, water or river organisms have developed special features to suit their habitat (e.g. large floating leaves, tall stems, webbed feet, waterproof feathers, good swimmers, etc). Think about the following river animals. How are they suited to their habitat? Draw and label the features.

  a trout   c otter
  b swan   d dragonfly

3 Work with a group of friends and make a collage of a river to show its different stages and what happens at each stage. Collect pictures of the water plants and animals, stick them in the correct places along the river, and label them. Discuss how each of the plants and animals is especially suited to its watery habitat. Your group could make a presentation to the class.

Only a few species of plants are able to survive in the mixture of salt and fresh water in an estuary.

Life in a wood

A wood has many plants growing in layers, which may include trees, shrubs, herbaceous (non-woody) plants, ferns, mosses and **fungi**. A wood is also home to many animals.

Purple Emperor butterfly

grey squirrel

fly agaric mushroom

millipede

The layers of growth in a deciduous woodland, and some of the animals that live there.

Woodland trees

Deciduous trees lose their leaves in autumn and grow new leaves the following spring. Oak, beech, larch and hickory are deciduous. **Evergreen** trees keep their leaves all the year round. Evergreens include Scots pine, eucalyptus, yew and holly.

The shrub and herb layers

Beneath the tree layer are shrubs and small trees. Underneath this shrub layer is a layer of ferns and flowering plants called the herb layer. Many woodland plants, such as wood anemones and primroses, grow and flower in the springtime. This is because sunlight can reach them only before the deciduous trees have developed their new leaves. When the trees open their leaves, the smaller plants die down and survive on stored food until the following spring.

The woodland floor

On the woodland floor there is often a layer of mosses and lichens. These simple plants need little light – they prefer damp, shady places. Rotting logs and dead leaves are home to many small animals such as beetles, woodlice, springtails, millipedes, centipedes and spiders. These animals need to stay cool, dark and damp so that they do not dry out and die. Fungi feed and grow on the fallen logs and branches and soften them as the wood rots away. Insects can then burrow into the rotting wood.

Bluebells are growing on this woodland floor.

Woodland animals

The tree layer is the habitat of many small insect-eating birds, such as tits and warblers. These feed on insects that eat the tree leaves. Woodpeckers feed on insects that live in rotting tree trunks and branches. Owls and sparrowhawks may sleep and nest in the taller trees but hunt for their prey in all parts of the wood.

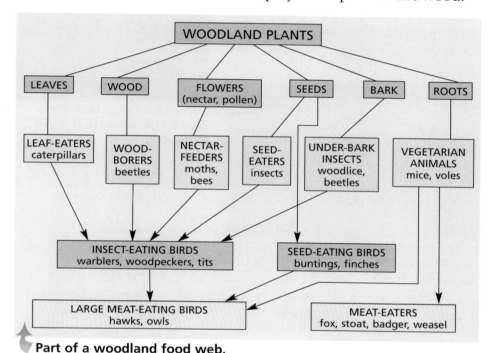

Part of a woodland food web.

Many larger animals live and feed in woodland. They include deer, badgers, foxes, weasels, mice, voles, shrews, hedgehogs and rabbits. With the large number of different animals and plants living in woodland, there are hundreds of food chains. They all start with the energy from sunlight, either in living plants or their dead remains.

Questions

1 Write down or draw a food chain from an area of woodland. For each of the living things in your food chain, say whether it is a producer, a primary consumer or a secondary consumer. Explain how each of the living things in your food chain is suited to its woodland habitat.

2 To help them to survive in their habitats, living things have developed special features to suit the place where they live. How are the following woodland animals suited to their habitat?

a squirrel
b woodpecker
c deer
d woodlouse

3 What kinds of woods and forests have the most wildlife in them: natural woods and forests of broad-leaved trees, or forests of conifers planted by people? Work with a friend and use reference material to find out. Make a class display or presentation of one type of woodland.

Soils and plant growth

There are many kinds of soil. Different types of soil are produced depending on the type of rock underneath and the climate of the area. The colour of the soil depends on how much **humus** (dead plant and animal material) there is in it and how much the rain has washed minerals out of the soil.

Soils formed in bogs and marshes where the ground is always wet are not very **fertile**. Because the ground is so wet, there is not enough air for plant roots to breathe properly.

Heather moorland is not very fertile because it is dry and sandy.

Cotton grass is one of the few plants that can grow on wet, boggy soils.

Sandy soils

Some soils are made of grains of rock that are just big enough to see. When you rub the soil between your fingers, you can feel the little grains. This is a sandy soil. A sandy soil is easy to dig and there is plenty of air in it for plant roots to breathe. When it rains, water runs through a sandy soil quickly. Sometimes in dry weather the plants growing on a sandy soil do not have enough water. Then they wilt and die.

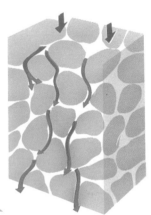

Water runs easily through a sandy soil.

Clay soils

Clay soils are made from pieces of rock so small that you cannot see them. If you rub the soil between your fingers it feels slippery like soap. You can form it into a ball. There is little air in a clay soil for plant roots to breathe. Digging clay soil is very hard work, particularly when it is wet. Water does not pass through a clay soil very easily, so a spadeful of clay soil is heavy. When the weather is dry, big cracks may form in a clay soil. Plant roots near these cracks often dry out and die.

Water does not run easily through a clay soil.

This lettuce crop is growing on fertile loam soil.

Loam soils

The best kind of soil is called a **loam**. It has as much clay as sand in it. It also contains a lot of humus. A loam is quite easy to dig and it does not dry out quickly in hot weather. Plants grow well in a loam soil and it is also home for many kinds of plants and animals. The most fertile loam soils are found under grassland and under the forests of broad-leaved trees such as oak and beech. These soils have taken thousands of years to form and they contain large amounts of humus.

Questions

1 Plan an experiment to compare how well seeds grow in a clay soil, a sandy soil and a loam soil.

   a What do you think will happen?
   b What kinds of seeds will you use? Why?
   c How will you make sure that your experiment is fair?
   d What measurements will you make?
   e How will you record your results?

Try out your experiment to see whether it works. Could it be improved?

2 a Make a class list of as many things as you can that grow in the soil. Try to think of one for each letter of the alphabet.
   b Now try to prepare a similar (but smaller) list of animals that live in the soil.
   c Discuss your list with a friend. What features do these soil animals have in common?

3 All soils contain water. Plan an experiment to compare how much water there is in two different samples of soil. What will you do? What measurements will you make? How will you make your experiment fair?

Animal and plant groups

There are animals and plants everywhere. Over 1 million different **species**, or kinds of animals, have been named, and at least 400 000 species of plants. There are also believed to be many more species of plants and animals that have not been discovered yet.

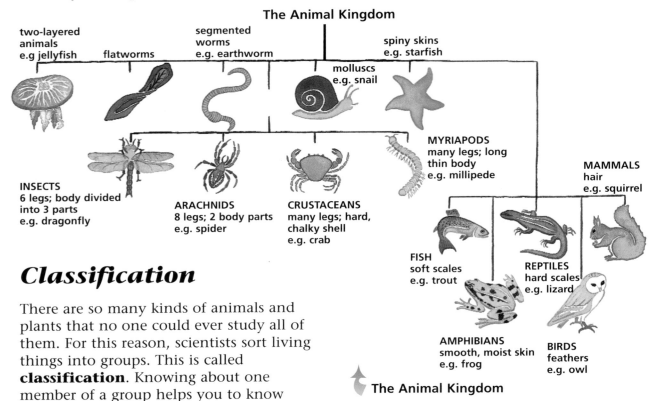

The Animal Kingdom

two-layered animals e.g jellyfish

flatworms

segmented worms e.g. earthworm

molluscs e.g. snail

spiny skins e.g. starfish

INSECTS 6 legs; body divided into 3 parts e.g. dragonfly

ARACHNIDS 8 legs; 2 body parts e.g. spider

CRUSTACEANS many legs; hard, chalky shell e.g. crab

MYRIAPODS many legs; long thin body e.g. millipede

MAMMALS hair e.g. squirrel

FISH soft scales e.g. trout

REPTILES hard scales e.g. lizard

AMPHIBIANS smooth, moist skin e.g. frog

BIRDS feathers e.g. owl

The Animal Kingdom

Classification

There are so many kinds of animals and plants that no one could ever study all of them. For this reason, scientists sort living things into groups. This is called **classification**. Knowing about one member of a group helps you to know more about the others.

Animal groups

Scientists sort animals into two big groups: **vertebrates** and **invertebrates**. A vertebrate is an animal with a backbone. Many animals, including humans, have a skeleton of bone with a backbone inside their body. Horses, cows, mice, birds, snakes, frogs and fish all have a backbone made up of several smaller bones called vertebrae. There are over 50 000 species of vertebrates. They are, in turn, put into five large groups called **mammals**, **birds**, **reptiles**, **amphibians** and **fish**.

An invertebrate is an animal without a backbone. These are animals like crabs, lobsters, jellyfish, butterflies, moths, slugs, snails, woodlice and spiders. Some of them have a shell or tough skin on the outside, but they do not have a skeleton and backbone inside their bodies. The invertebrate group, in turn, is divided into smaller groups such as insects, crustaceans (crabs, lobsters and shrimps), worms, and arachnids (spiders and scorpions).

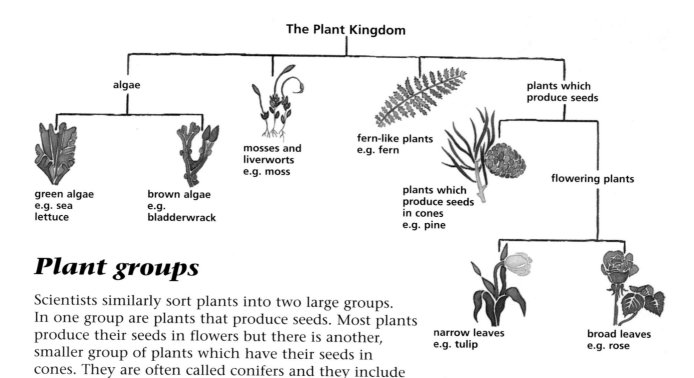

The Plant Kingdom

algae

green algae
e.g. sea
lettuce

brown algae
e.g.
bladderwrack

mosses and
liverworts
e.g. moss

fern-like plants
e.g. fern

plants which
produce seeds

plants which
produce seeds
in cones
e.g. pine

flowering plants

narrow leaves
e.g. tulip

broad leaves
e.g. rose

The Plant Kingdom

Plant groups

Scientists similarly sort plants into two large groups. In one group are plants that produce seeds. Most plants produce their seeds in flowers but there is another, smaller group of plants which have their seeds in cones. They are often called conifers and they include pine, larch, spruce, fir, and yew trees. In the other group are the plants that produce new plants from tiny dust-like **spores**. Among these plants are the ferns, mosses, liverworts, and algae or seaweeds.

Questions

1 a Classify the living things in the box into plants and animals. Make a table of the two lists.
   b Now divide your list of plants into smaller groups and your list of animals into smaller groups.
   c Compare your lists with those of your friends. How many groups have you made?

| grass   seaweed   earthworm   jellyfish |
| oak tree   goldfish   horse   housefly |
| sunflower   pine tree   moss   dragonfly |
| snake   lettuce   fern   mouse   eagle |
| woodlouse   buttercup |

2 Make a list of all the invertebrate animals you can think of which have a shell on the outside of their body. How many ways can you find of dividing these animals into smaller groups or sets?

3 Read the following sentences. Which group of animals is being described by each sentence? Use the Glossary and the Animal Kingdom classification to help you.

   a Cold blooded; scaly skin; lay their eggs on land.
   b Eight legs; no backbone.
   c Hairy; feed their young on milk; warm blooded.
   d Six legs; no backbone.
   e Fins; cold-blooded; scaly skin; live in water.

Using keys

Keys are a useful way to sort animals and plants into their correct groups. Scientists can use keys to identify unknown plants or animals.

Types of key

A key uses differences between a collection of plants or animals to split them into smaller and smaller groups. A key consists of a series of questions, each with two possible answers. The answers lead you to the next question or to the name of the unknown plant or animal. There are two kinds of key. Branching keys are most useful when there are only a few plants or animals to be identified. Numbered keys are most useful when there are large numbers of plants or animals to be sorted.

Using a key

Here is a simple branching key to separate six common tree leaves:

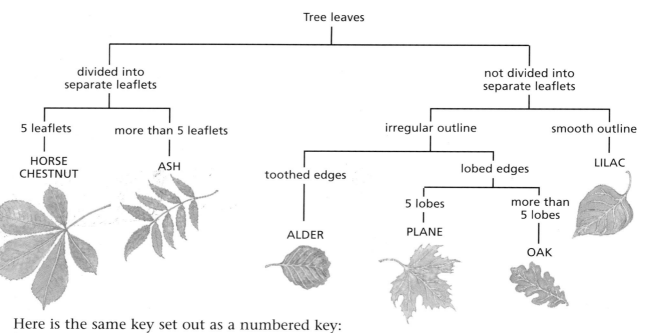

Here is the same key set out as a numbered key:

1	Divided into separate leaflets Not divided into separate leaflets	see 2 see 3
2	5 leaflets More than 5 leaflets	HORSE CHESTNUT ASH
3	Smooth outline Irregular outline	LILAC see 4
4	Toothed edges Lobed edges	ALDER see 5
5	5 lobes More than 5 lobes	PLANE OAK

Here is a simple numbered key to separate the five groups of vertebrate animals:

1	Animals with fins Animals with no fins	FISH see 2
2	Animals with feathers Animals with no feathers	BIRDS see 3
3	Animals with hair or fur Animals with no hair or fur	MAMMALS see 4
4	Animals with dry, scaly skin Animals with moist, smooth skin	REPTILES AMPHIBIANS

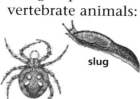
slug

spider

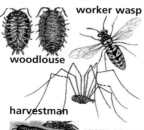
snail

This numbered key will help you to identify the main groups of invertebrate animals that you may find in the garden or school grounds:

1	Animals with soft bodies and no legs Animals with hard bodies and legs	see 2 see 4
2	Long body divided into rings or segments Body not divided into rings or segments	EARTHWORMS see 3
3	4 tentacles with external (outside) shell 4 tentacles with no external shell	SNAILS SLUGS
4	Body with more than 14 pairs of legs Body with fewer than 14 pairs of legs	see 5 see 6
5	Body flattened, with 2 legs per segment Body flattened, with 4 legs per segment	CENTIPEDE MILLIPEDE
6	7 pairs of legs, body grey or steely blue Fewer than 7 pairs of legs	WOODLOUSE see 7
7	4 pairs of legs 3 pairs of legs and a body in 3 parts	see 8 INSECTS
8	Body divided into 2 parts Body not divided, legs extremely long and hair-like	SPIDERS HARVESTMEN

worker wasp

woodlouse

harvestman

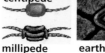
centipede

millipede   earthworm

Questions

bus   aeroplane   bicycle   car
motor boat

Do these exercises in pairs or small groups. You can use a computer and suitable software to construct your keys.

1 Make a branching key to identify the five forms of transport in the box.

   Begin by asking a question which has the answer 'yes' or 'no' for each object. For example, you could ask the question 'Does it have wheels?'

2 a Write out the numbered key of vertebrate animals (above), this time as a branching key.
   b Now do the same for the invertebrate animals key.

3 Produce a branching or numbered key to identify a group of five or six of your friends. What features will you use to separate them? Remember they do not always wear the same clothes.

Solutions

When a substance **dissolves** in a liquid, a **solution** is made. Seawater is a solution of salt and other substances in water. Fizzy drinks contain, amongst other things, the gas carbon dioxide dissolved in water, while fish breathe oxygen that is dissolved in the water around them. Liquids will dissolve in liquids: for example, oil dissolves in petrol. It is even possible to 'dissolve' a solid in a solid. Brass, for example, is made by dissolving copper metal in molten zinc metal.

soluble aspirin

washing-up liquid

soap

bath salts

soy sauce

coffee granules

sugar

salt

These substances are soluble in water.

Soluble and insoluble

Substances that dissolve are said to be **soluble**. Those which do not dissolve are called **insoluble**. The liquid in which a substance dissolves to form a solution is called a **solvent**. The substance that dissolves is a **solute**.

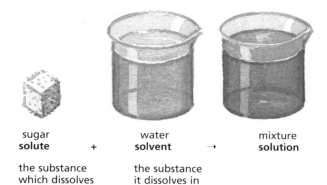

sugar
solute
the substance which dissolves

+

water
solvent
the substance it dissolves in

→

mixture
solution

What is a solution?

All solutions of a solid in a liquid contain two parts. There is the liquid part, the solvent, and the dissolved substance, or solute.

If you put a teaspoon of sugar in a glass of water, the sugar seems to disappear and you have a sugar solution. A sip of the liquid tells you that the sugar is still there. In this example, water is the solvent and the sugar is the solute.

Particles

Water is made of very tiny particles, while sugar is made of slightly larger particles. The water particles are close together and always moving. They have small spaces between them.

When you add sugar to water, the small water particles get between the larger sugar particles. If you add a teaspoon of sugar to a glass of water, all the sugar will dissolve. If you now add more and more sugar, eventually no more sugar will dissolve. You now have what is called a **saturated solution**. Some substances are very soluble and a lot of them will dissolve in a certain amount of liquid. Other substances are only slightly soluble.

You can get a dissolved substance back again by heating the solution so that the liquid **evaporates** away. If you stand a saucer of sugar solution on a sunny windowsill or near a radiator, the water will eventually evaporate away leaving the sugar on the saucer.

Evaporating a sugar solution leaves sugar behind.

In some hot countries, like Thailand, people collect seawater in shallow ponds near the shore. Then the sun's heat makes the water evaporate, leaving the salt behind.

Questions

1 The words in the box all have something to do with dissolving. For each one, explain in your own words what it means.

> soluble   solute   solvent
> insoluble   solution

2 Look at the pairs of materials in the list on the right. Will any change take place when the pairs of materials are mixed together? Discuss your answers with a friend.

a salt and water
b sand and water
c oil and water
d soil and stones
e coffee and water
f rice and lentils

3 In some parts of the world there are deep underground beds of salt. Water is pumped down to the salt and then pumped back to the surface again. Discuss with a friend why this is done, and what you think happens next. Give reasons for your answers.

Dissolving more, dissolving faster

How much of a solute (or substance) dissolves depends on how much solvent you use. If you use more water or some other solvent to dissolve a solute such as salt or sugar, more salt or sugar can be added until the solution is saturated. You will know when that has happened because some of the salt or sugar will remain undissolved at the bottom of the container.

Making more solute dissolve

However much solvent you use, more solute will dissolve if you warm the solvent. This means that, for example, more sugar will dissolve in warm water than in cold water (picture B). When the solvent is warmed, the tiny particles it is made of move faster. This increases the spaces between them so that there is room for more solute to dissolve. Most solids dissolve better in warm water than in cold water. Salt is one of the few substances where there is little change in the amount which dissolves as the temperature of the water rises.

Some substances can be dissolved in water and used to dye fabric and wool. These dyeing pits are in Morocco.

Making the solute dissolve faster

If you put a soluble solid, such as sugar, into a solvent, it may take a long time to dissolve. If you stir the mixture, the sugar will dissolve more quickly (picture A). This is because stirring mixes up the particles of solvent and solute so that they are more spread out. Stirring does not increase the amount of solute that dissolves, it simply makes it dissolve faster.

Most soluble solid substances dissolve faster if they are first ground up before they are put into the solvent. You can see this for yourself if you put granulated sugar into one beaker of water and the same amount of cube sugar into another identical beaker of water (picture C). Grinding or crushing the solid increases the area of it which is exposed to the solvent so that it dissolves faster.

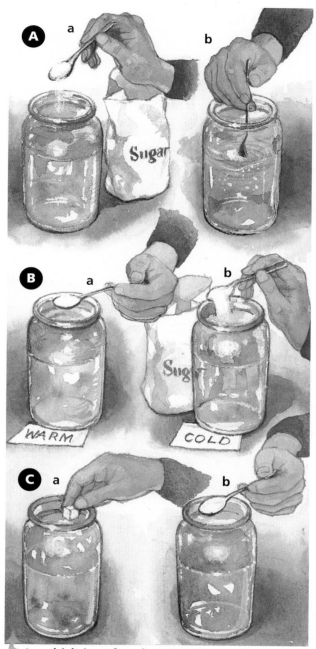

In which jar of each pair will the sugar dissolve faster?

A a: not stirred   b: stirred

B a: warm water   b: cold water

C a: cube sugar   b: granulated sugar

Questions

1 Carol took a glass of water out of the fridge. She added five teaspoons of sugar to the water. No matter how much she stirred the mixture, some grains of sugar remained in the water. Without adding any more water, how could Carol make all the sugar dissolve?

2 a Describe three things you could do to make sugar dissolve faster. Draw pictures and label what you would do in each case.

   b How could you get the sugar back from the solution? How could you speed up this process?

3 Plan an investigation to compare how much salt dissolves in 100 cm³ of water and how much sugar dissolves in 100 cm³ of water.

   a What do you think will happen?
   b Think of at least two ways you could measure the amount of salt and sugar.
   c How will you make sure your investigation is fair?
   d Try out your investigation. Do you think your results are accurate? How could you make them more accurate?

Cells, batteries and circuits

A **battery** uses chemicals to produce electricity. The battery turns chemical energy into electrical energy. The proper name for a single battery like the one in the picture is an electric **cell**. When the cell is joined up in a complete **circuit**, the chemicals in the cell produce an electric current. The word 'battery' really means two or more cells joined together. A cell provides an electrical force that pushes electricity around the circuit. The strength of this electrical force is measured in units called **volts**. Most electrical cells produce an electrical force of one and a half volts (1.5V). If a number of cells are joined together, they make a battery. Two cells joined together produce three volts, while a 9-volt battery, like the one in the picture, consists of six cells joined together.

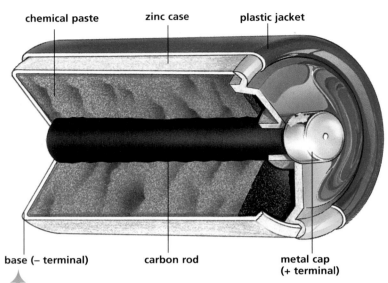

chemical paste   zinc case   plastic jacket

base (– terminal)   carbon rod   metal cap (+ terminal)

Inside a single cell of the kind used in torches.

Circuits

If you connect a bulb and a cell in a complete circuit, the bulb lights. This circuit is a loop with no beginning and no end.

Electricity moves, or flows, around the whole circuit. It flows through the wires, the bulb and the cell. The arrows in the circuit on the next page show the way it flows. You cannot see the electricity in a circuit like this; you can see only what it does. When electricity flows it makes the bulb light. Energy from the cell is needed to make electricity flow around the circuit. This energy, which has been stored in the cell, is changed to heat and light in the bulb.

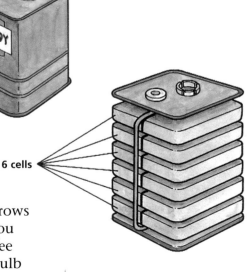

EVEREADY

6 cells

Inside a 9-volt battery.

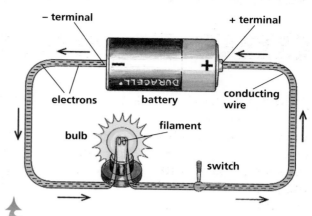

A simple circuit with a switch.

Switches

To turn an electric light on or off, you normally use a switch. A switch is a way of opening and closing a gap in a circuit. Using a switch is easier and safer than touching two wires together or pulling them apart.

In an electric light circuit, it does not matter on which side of the bulb you connect a switch. Electricity that flows through the bulb must also flow through the switch. Electricity flows through the bulb only when the switch is 'on' and the gap in the circuit is closed. When the switch is 'off', there is a gap in the circuit and the electricity cannot flow.

Batteries are safe to touch because they are low power, but mains electricity is dangerous and can kill you.

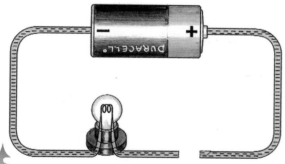

There is a gap in this circuit. Electricity cannot flow across the gap so the bulb will not light.

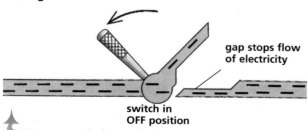

gap stops flow of electricity

switch in OFF position

How a switch works to open and close a gap in a circuit.

Questions

1 Imagine you have made a simple circuit using a battery, a switch, three wires and a bulb. The bulb doesn't light up. What might be wrong? Think of four things and describe them or draw diagrams.

2 Sanjay's mother asked him to get the washing in if it rained, but Sanjay wanted to watch the television. How could he make something to let him know when it is raining outside? In a small group, design a circuit Sanjay could make, using a cell or battery.

3 Design a set of model traffic lights. Remember the lights work in order, starting with red at the top, then amber, then green. When the lights are going back from green to red, they go to red and amber, and then to red.

  a What materials do you need?
  b If you are able to obtain them all, make your model. Does it work?
  c How could you improve your model?

Drawing circuits

Scientists often draw diagrams to show electrical circuits. They use **symbols** instead of pictures of the parts of the circuit. This saves time and it is a good way to show someone how a circuit should be connected up.

Here are some of the symbols that scientists use:

Component	Picture	Symbol
Cell		
Two cells		
Bulb		or
Buzzer		
Motor		M
Switch-off		
Switch-on		

In a circuit diagram you do not need to draw the connecting wires the right shape, thickness or length. You only show how they are connected up, and straight lines look neater than wiggly ones!

Here is a drawing of a simple circuit with a bulb, cell and switch:

Here is a diagram of the same circuit, first of all with the switch 'off' and then with the switch 'on':

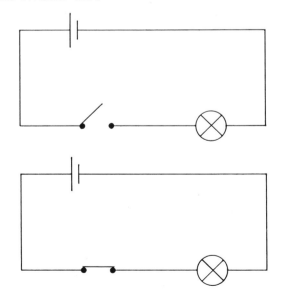

Terminals

A cell or battery has two ends, called **terminals**. Electricity flows from the negative (–) terminal to the positive (+) terminal of the cell or battery. The electricity can flow from the negative terminal to the positive terminal only if they are joined by a material that conducts electricity, such as a wire or some other piece of metal. On a circuit diagram the long vertical line on the symbol is the positive (+) terminal and the shorter vertical line is the negative (–) terminal. When two or more cells are connected together you can link the individual cell symbols together, as shown in the chart opposite.

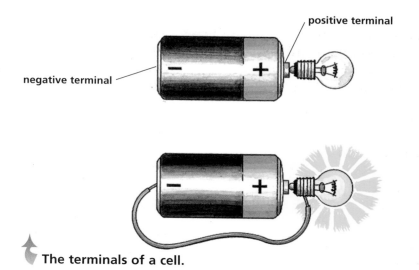

positive terminal

negative terminal

The terminals of a cell.

Circuit diagram rules

When you draw circuit diagrams remember these simple rules:

- Electricity has to flow from the negative terminal of the cell or battery and back to the positive terminal for the circuit to work.

- No electricity will flow if there is a gap in the circuit.

- There has to be a component, such as a bulb, buzzer or motor in the circuit.

Questions

1 How does a torch work? Draw the circuit, using symbols, and describe it to a friend.

2 a Draw a circuit diagram, showing a circuit with a cell, wires, an open switch and a bulb.
  b Now learn the symbols. How well can you remember them? With a friend, test each other.

3 a Draw a circuit diagram showing a circuit with two cells, wires, an open switch and an electric motor.
  b Try to find a circuit diagram of an electrical item that you have at home, for example an iron or a hair-drier. Which symbols can you find? Can you draw any of the circuits?

4 Draw a circuit diagram of a cell connected to two bulbs. There is a switch between the cell and one of the bulbs. What object might have this circuit?

Brighter and dimmer

Did you know that you can light more than one bulb with one cell? The diagram on the right shows one way of doing this. In this circuit electricity flows through each of the bulbs. The bulbs are said to be wired in series.

Series circuits

The more bulbs you add to a **series circuit** like this, the dimmer each bulb will be. You might expect the bulb nearest the cell to be brighter than the others. It isn't, and this is because the bulbs share the electricity which comes from the cell. Many series circuits are used in televisions and computers, but series circuits have one big disadvantage. If there is a break anywhere in the circuit, as, for example, when one of the bulbs blows, then the whole circuit is broken.

Parallel circuits

There is another way of lighting several bulbs with one cell. In this kind of circuit, called a **parallel circuit**, some electricity flows through each bulb. The bulbs are then brighter than they would be if they were connected in series. If you unscrew one bulb in a parallel circuit, the others will stay alight, because each has its own separate circuit to the cell. The electric lights in your home and school are connected in a parallel circuit like this.

Extra cells

Often several cells are used in a circuit. Like bulbs, cells can be connected in different ways. Usually they are connected in series. Either a wire connects the bottom of one cell to the top of the next or, as in a torch, the cells actually touch each other.

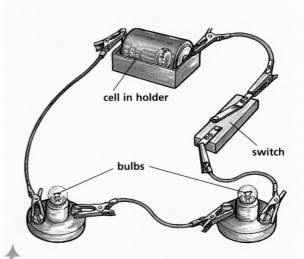

The bulbs in this circuit are in series. If one bulb is removed the other goes out.

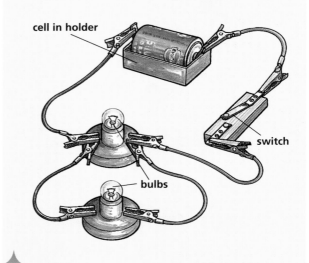

The bulbs in this circuit are in parallel. If one bulb is removed the other stays alight since it has its own separate circuit.

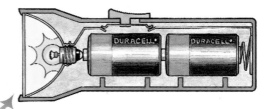

A torch with two cells connected in series.

Two cells connected in series light a bulb more brightly than just one cell. Adding more cells in series makes the bulb light even brighter. Doing this may make the bulb 'burn out' more quickly. The filament or tiny wire inside the bulb will glow so brightly that it melts and breaks the circuit. Bulbs are made for a certain number of cells. If they are connected to more cells than they are made for, they quickly 'burn out'.

Varying the current

You can also change the amount of electricity flowing through a circuit by adding longer wires. Long, thin wires allow less electricity to flow through them than short, thick wires made of the same material. How much electricity flows also depends on what the wires are made of. More electric current will flow through a copper wire than through an iron wire of the same size. The amount by which a wire or any other object cuts down the electricity flowing through it is called its **resistance**.

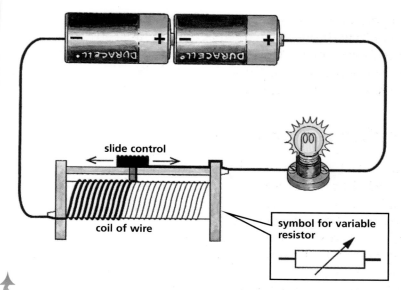

slide control

coil of wire

symbol for variable resistor

This device is called a variable resistor. It changes the length of wire in a circuit so that the bulb can be made brighter or dimmer.

Questions

1 How would you make a bulb in a circuit shine with a dimmer light? Think of two ways.

2 a Which of the objects and materials in the box would allow an electric current to pass through them? Explain why.
  b In a small group, make a circuit and experiment to test your answers.

brass	iron nail	plastic pot	steel paper clip
glass rod	rubber	wooden ruler	soap	gold ring
copper coin	tin lid

3 a How could you make a model room with two working lights so that if one bulb is removed the other stays alight? Draw a circuit diagram of your model room.
  b Make your model and see if it works.
  c How could you improve your design?

4 Draw circuit diagrams of the four circuits shown on these two pages.

Useful electricity

Electricity is a form of energy we use every day. In our homes and schools we turn electricity into other kinds of energy. Electrical energy is turned into light and heat in light bulbs and electric fires. It is turned into sound energy in telephones, televisions, personal stereos, doorbells and burglar alarms, for example. Electric motors turn electrical energy into mechanical or movement energy. Electricity is very easy to control, and it is there at the flick of a switch.

Light bulbs

Whenever electricity flows it heats up the material it flows through. Inside a light bulb the filament, a very thin, coiled wire, has a high resistance to electricity. When electricity flows through the filament, the thin wire becomes so hot that it glows and gives out light. The bulb is filled with a special gas that stops the filament from burning away too quickly. A torch bulb works in a similar way.

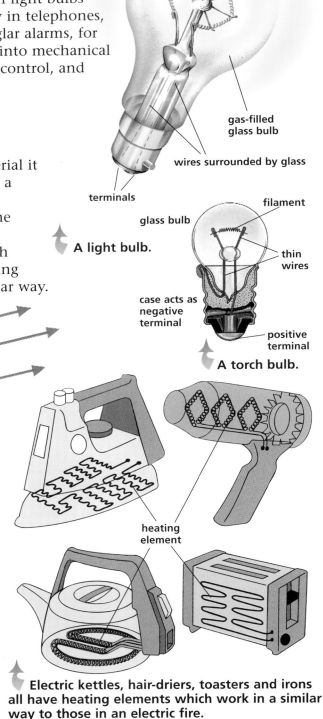

filament

gas-filled glass bulb

wires surrounded by glass

terminals

A light bulb.

glass bulb

filament

thin wires

case acts as negative terminal

positive terminal

A torch bulb.

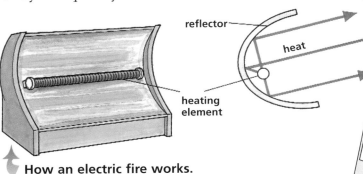

reflector

heat

heating element

How an electric fire works.

Electric heaters

The glowing element of an electric fire is a long piece of thin wire made of a metal called nichrome. This wire has a high resistance and it is wound around a rod made of an **insulator** such as fireclay. When electricity flows through the nichrome wire, the wire gets very hot. A shiny metal reflector helps to radiate the heat into the room. The wire used in the cable leading to the electric fire is made of thick copper. Because it has a much lower resistance to electricity it does not get hot.

heating element

Electric kettles, hair-driers, toasters and irons all have heating elements which work in a similar way to those in an electric fire.

Mains electricity is dangerous and can kill you. Never remove the plastic cover of a plug or other electrical equipment.

Fuses

There are times when the heat given out by an electric current is dangerous. If there is a fault in an electrical circuit, or if an accident occurs, too much electricity can flow through a wire or cable. It can start a fire. Delicate electrical machines can also be damaged. To stop these things happening, there are **fuses** near the meter, where electric cables come into a building. There are also fuses in plugs and in machines connected to the mains.

A fuse is a thin wire with a low melting point that is part of an electrical circuit. If the right amount of electricity is flowing around the circuit, it can go through the fuse without difficulty. If too much electricity flows, the fuse heats up and quickly melts. It makes a gap in the circuit, which stops the electricity flowing.

There are fuses like these in plugs and in machines connected to the mains.

Questions

1 a Draw a picture of a light bulb, or copy the picture of a light bulb on the opposite page. Label your picture.
   b Is each part a conductor or an insulator? Make a table of your answers.

2 a Make a list of all the appliances in your home that turn electrical energy into heat or light.
   b What sort of fuse does each appliance have? Ask an adult or look for a label on the appliance when it is switched off – don't try to look inside!

3 a Design a model lighthouse with a light that you can make flash on and off. Base your model on a clean plastic drinks bottle.
   b Make a circuit drawing of your lighthouse.
   c Make your model.
   d How could you improve it?
   e Use reference materials to find out what causes the light to turn in a real lighthouse. Why would it be difficult to get the bulb to turn around in your model lighthouse? Discuss this with a friend.

The power station

Most of the electricity we use in our homes, schools, shops and factories comes from a power station. In a **power station** are huge **generators** that produce electricity.

The turbines and generators inside a power station.

Inside a power station

Each generator in a power station consists of an enormous magnet surrounded by coils of copper wire. When the magnet is rotated very fast it produces electricity.

Most power stations burn a fuel, such as coal, oil or gas, or use a radioactive material, such as uranium, to produce heat. This heat is used to boil water and turn it into steam. The steam rushes through pipes to a large wheel fitted with blades, rather like a propeller. This wheel is called a **turbine**. As the steam flows past the blades of the turbine, it makes the turbine spin rapidly. As the turbine spins, it turns the generator which produces electricity.

Because it is difficult to store electricity, it must be made as it is needed. In cold weather and at busy times of the day most power stations have many turbines and generators working to produce electricity.

The National Grid

Electricity is carried from the power stations to cities, towns and villages by a network of wires covering the whole country. In Britain, this is called the **National Grid**. A power station produces electricity at 25 000 volts, but it is sent across the National Grid at 400 000 volts. Special devices called transformers are used to change the **voltage** of the electricity.

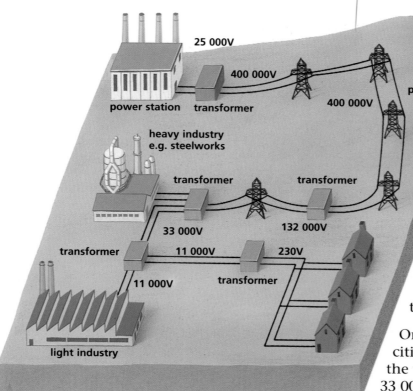

25 000V

400 000V

power station   transformer

400 000V

pylons

heavy industry
e.g. steelworks

transformer

transformer

33 000V

132 000V

transformer

11 000V

230V

11 000V

transformer

light industry

The National Grid brings electricity to your home.

From the transformer the electricity is taken across the country on overhead wires made of aluminium, because this metal is a good **conductor** of electricity. These wires are carried on tall steel towers called pylons. The wires are hung on porcelain or glass holders because these materials are good insulators and stop the electricity from escaping down the pylons to the ground.

On the outskirts of towns and cities more transformers change the voltage of the electricity, first to 33 000 volts and then to 11 000 volts. Factories take their electricity at these voltages. Near houses, more transformers reduce the voltage to 230 volts and underground cables take the electricity to homes, shops and schools.

Questions

1 In which ways does a large supermarket use electricity? Discuss this in small groups, then draw and label a picture of the supermarket to show where electricity is used.

2 Where is the power station nearest to your home or school? Is it near a river, lake or the sea? What kind of fuel does it use, or how else does it obtain its energy?

3 The rate at which things use electricity is measured in watts or kilowatts (a kilowatt is 1000 watts). On a light bulb, for example, you might see written 60 watts (or 60W) or 100 watts (100W); on a vacuum cleaner, say, 1200 watts (1200W).

a Look around your home for objects which are powered by electricity. How much electricity does each one use?

b Make a table to record the rate at which each object uses electricity.

c Which objects in your home use most electricity? Which objects use least electricity?

Generating electricity without fuel

Using coal, oil, gas or nuclear fuels is not the only way to produce electricity. Supplies of coal, oil and gas will not last for ever and these fuels can pollute the air, producing acid rain, and adding to global warming. Nuclear power stations can also cause dangerous pollution if radioactive material accidentally leaks out, and the radioactive waste is dangerous and difficult to dispose of. There are other, cleaner ways of producing electricity, which do not use fuels and which will not run out. They are said to be renewable.

Hydro-electricity

Electricity can be made by using running water to spin turbines and generators to make electricity. This electricity is produced in a **hydro-electric power** station. Water from a fast-flowing river on a hillside or mountain may be carried by pipes into the power station. Some hydro-electric power stations are built inside a dam. Water passes through the dam under great pressure and turns the turbines and generators on its way.

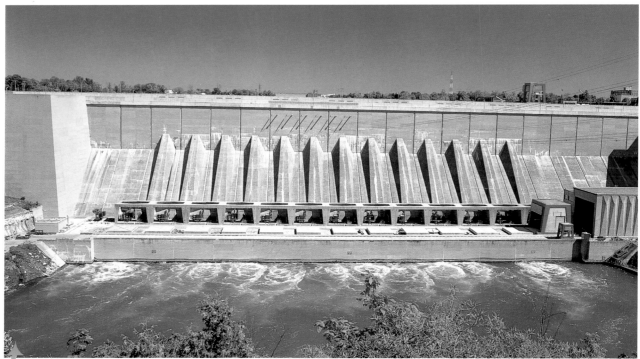

This hydro-electric power station at Niagara, North America, uses the energy of running water to turn the generators.

In France there is a power station which uses the energy of the moving water of the tides. As the tide comes in or goes out of the river estuary, the moving water turns underwater turbines and generators that produce electricity. In a few places there are power stations that use the waves of the sea to drive their generators.

Turbines on this wind farm in California use the energy of the wind to produce electricity.

Wind energy

The energy of the wind has been used for hundreds of years to grind corn, pump water or drive machinery. In recent years new types of wind turbines have been developed. As their blades turn in the wind they drive generators to produce electricity.

Energy from the sun and from rocks

Solar power stations change sunlight into electricity. Some use solar cells rather like the ones in solar-powered calculators. In countries such as Iceland, Italy, New Zealand and the United States, there are hot rocks not too far below the surface of the Earth. Sometimes there are also hot springs which shoot steam or hot water into the air. In some of these places, the steam or hot water from underground is used to drive generators that produce electricity.

This power station in Sicily uses the sun's energy to produce electricity.

Questions

1 What do you think are the advantages and disadvantages of these ways of producing electricity?

   a hydro-electric power stations
   b solar power stations
   c wind turbines

   Discuss this in small groups, then make a table of your results.

2 Which renewable source of energy do you think would be best for supplying electricity to your area? Use reference material, such as books, CD-ROMs and the Internet, to find out more about that source. Make a presentation to the class.

3 Mains electricity can be dangerous, however it is produced. Design and make a poster to warn people of the dangers of working with or near electricity.

Gravity

Gravity is the **force** that pulls all objects towards the centre of the Earth. The reason that things fall to the ground is because of gravity. It is also gravity that keeps you firmly on the ground.

Isaac Newton

It is said that about 300 years ago an apple fell from a tree onto the head of Isaac Newton, a great English scientist. Newton realized that the apple fell because of the Earth's pull. It was Isaac Newton who discovered gravity.

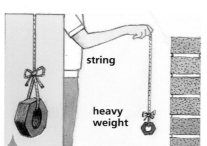

Builders can use a plumbline to see that a wall is vertical. The weight on the plumbline pulls the string towards the centre of the Earth, so the plumbline hangs vertically.

Feeling the pull of gravity

If you hold your arm outstretched with a heavy book in your hand, you can feel the pull of gravity. The **weight** of the book pushing down on your hand is due to the pull of gravity. Your body, like everything else on the Earth, weighs something because of the pull of gravity. Gravity stops you floating off the Earth into space, and makes a ball you throw up into the air come down again.

The athlete jumps up, but is pulled back down to Earth by gravity.

Falling objects

If a heavy object and a light object are dropped at the same time, they both hit the ground together. Gravity makes all things fall equally fast. This was discovered about 400 years ago by the great Italian scientist, Galileo. Galileo dropped balls of different weights from the leaning tower of Pisa in Italy. They all hit the ground at the same time.

Gravity on the moon

The moon is much smaller than the Earth and its gravity is only about one-sixth as strong as the Earth's gravity. This means that astronauts on the moon weigh only about one-sixth as much as they do on Earth. It is easy for them to take giant strides as they walk, and they can jump six times as high as they would be able to on Earth.

This astronaut takes a giant leap on the moon.

Questions

1 How has gravity affected you today? Write a sentence about each of the ways, and draw and label diagrams to help your explanation.

2 Ashley throws his ball straight up into the air. Draw Ashley and the ball.

 a What happens to the speed of the ball as it goes up?
 b Why does the ball fall down again? The Earth's pull, or gravity, and air resistance act on the ball as it falls. Mark these forces on your drawing.
 c Which force is bigger, the Earth's pull or air resistance?
 d How do you know?

3 Find and look at pictures of tree seeds which fly as they fall from trees. They include ash, sycamore, maple and lime. Plan an investigation to find out which wing shape is best for seed dispersal – that is, one which keeps the seed in the air for the longest time.

 a Which wing shape do you think will be best?
 b What materials will you use?
 c Where will you carry out your investigation?
 d What measurements will you make?
 e How will you record your results?
 f How will you make sure that your investigation is fair? Try out your investigation.
 g Could you make your results more accurate?

Measuring forces

Engineers and architects need to measure how strong a force is. They compare two or more forces and work out what effect they will have. It is particularly important to know the size of forces on large structures such as buildings, bridges and tunnels.

Newtons

You cannot see forces, but you can see what they do. You can see something speeding up, slowing down, changing direction or changing shape because of a force. You can also see how strong a force is by looking at what effect it has.

We measure forces in units called **newtons** (N), using a force meter or a newton meter. Inside this meter is a spring which is stretched by the force pulling on it. The bigger the force, the more the spring is stretched. The bigger the force the meter has to measure, the stronger the spring it has inside it. On the Earth, the weight of a 100 gram bar of chocolate is about one newton.

A force of 1 newton.

Weighing machines

Weighing machines measure the force of gravity pulling an object towards the centre of the Earth. Most weighing machines that you see every day in kitchens, bathrooms and shops have a scale, which shows kilograms (kg) and grams (g), not newtons. These machines are not really measuring force or weight, but **mass**.

These so-called weighing machines really measure mass.

Mass and weight

Most people use the word 'weight' when they really should be talking about 'mass'. The important thing to remember is that mass is a measure of the amount of material in something, while weight is the force of gravity acting on an object. On the Earth your mass might be 30 kg and your weight about 300 N (1 kilogram is about 10 newtons). If you went to the moon your mass would still be 30 kg (unless a piece of you dropped off on the way!), but your weight would be different. This is because the pull of gravity on the moon is only about one-sixth as strong as the pull of the Earth's gravity. As a result, on the moon your weight would be only about 50 N.

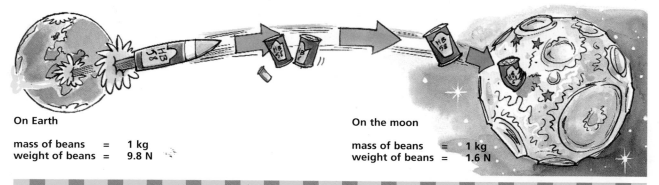

On Earth

mass of beans   =   1 kg
weight of beans =   9.8 N

On the moon

mass of beans   =   1 kg
weight of beans =   1.6 N

Questions

1 a What is the difference between mass and weight?
  b What is the weight of a kilogram of rice in newtons?

2 True or False? Copy out the sentences below. Write 'True' next to those statements you think are correct. Write 'False' next to those statements you think are wrong.

  a Gravity is a pulling force.
  b The mass of an object always stays the same.
  c An Italian scientist called Galileo discovered gravity.
  d Weight is measured in newtons.
  e The moon's gravity is less than the Earth's gravity.
  f Gravity is invisible.
  g You would weigh more on the moon than you do on Earth.

3 In small groups, plan an investigation to measure the force needed to pull different objects across a table.

  a How would you carry out this investigation if you did not have a newton meter?
  b What equipment would you need?
  c What measurements would you make?
  d How would you make sure that your investigation was fair and that your results were accurate?
  Try out your ideas to see if they work. Record your results in a line graph.
  e What did you find?

4 Make a class collection of various weighing machines. Examine them to see how they work.

  a What have you discovered?
  b For one of the machines, write instructions for a friend who does not know how to use the machine and draw diagrams to show how it works.

How to beat gravity

You already know that gravity pulls all objects down towards the centre of the Earth. Gravity pulls you down whether you are in the air, in water or simply standing on the ground, but there are several ways in which you can beat gravity.

An aircraft's engines and the special shape of its wings provide lift, which is greater than gravity.

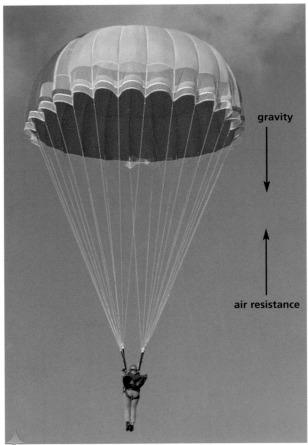

gravity

air resistance

▲ **A parachute comes down to the ground slowly because of the air resistance on it. Without the parachute, the person would plummet to the ground.**

Exerting a force

One way to beat gravity is to exert a force greater than the pull of gravity. When a bird is flying, its wings push against the air and provide an upward force called lift, which is greater than the force of gravity. A spacecraft has to have extremely powerful rocket motors that will thrust it completely beyond the force of the Earth's gravity into deep space.

Reducing gravity's effects

Sometimes you do not want to beat the force of gravity, but to reduce its effects. If you have ever ridden a bicycle you will know that air slows you down as you move through it. You feel as if you are pushing your way through the air because of this air resistance. If you jumped out of an aeroplane you would fall rapidly to the ground, because the pull of gravity is much larger than the air resistance on your body. If you jumped out of an aeroplane with a large parachute, you would drift slowly to the ground. The air resistance would be nearly as great as the pull of gravity.

Floating and sinking

When you float in water you weigh less than you do in air. This is because water pushes upwards and cancels out some of the force of gravity pulling down.

You can feel the **upthrust** of water if you put a large ball in a bowl or bucket of water. If you push down on the ball you can feel the force of the water pushing the ball back upwards. If you let go of the ball it may jump out of the water.

A heavy brick sinks in water because the pull of gravity is greater than the upthrust of the water. The upthrust is not very great because the brick only displaces, or pushes aside, a small amount of water. The brick is very heavy for its size or, as a scientist would say, it is very **dense**. A light cork floats in a beaker of water because the upthrust of the water on the cork balances the force of gravity on the cork.

Although a large ship may be made of steel it has many hollow parts with air in them. The ship displaces a huge quantity of water so that the upthrust of the water balances the pull of gravity on the ship, and the ship floats. If you could roll all the steel in a large ship into a ball and place this in water, it would displace much less water and the giant steel ball would sink.

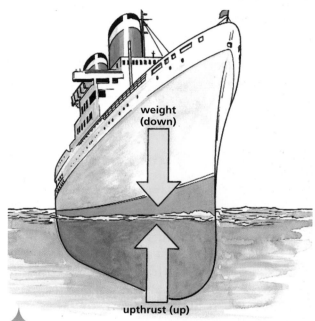

The ship floats because its weight and the upthrust force balance each other.

Questions

1 What two forces are acting on a rubber duck floating in bathwater? Draw a diagram and show the forces acting on the duck.

2 If you use some modelling clay to make a large boat shape, it will float. If you roll the same amount of modelling clay into a ball, it will sink. Why is this?

3 Nadine set up a class exhibition. She weighed out 100 g of all the materials that sank, such as sand, stones and metal screws. She also weighed out 100 g of all the materials that floated. What differences do you think she saw between the various heaps?
Set up a class exhibition like Nadine's.

Balanced forces

There is often more than one force acting on an object at the same time. If an object is not moving and not changing speed or direction, then the forces acting on it are said to be balanced.

Equal and opposite forces

Although the boys are of different weights, the forces on this see-saw are balanced.

These forces are not balanced!

If two forces of the same size act upon an object in opposite directions, the forces are balanced so that they cancel each other. We can see this if two children who weigh the same sit on a see-saw at the same distance from the centre. They will then balance each other and the see-saw stays still.

When two teams have a tug-of-war, each side tries to pull the other over a line. As both teams pull, there are often times when neither side moves. The pulling force of one team exactly matches the pulling force of the other team in the opposite direction. The forces are balanced because they are equal and opposite.

When you stand on the bathroom scales, your body weight exerts a downward force. The spring in the bathroom scales exerts an upward force to balance it.

If the rope suddenly broke, what would happen to the two teams?

Balanced movement

Even if you are moving along, forces can still be balanced. If you pedal your bicycle along a flat surface, you soon produce a force that is equal to the force of **friction** between the tyres and the road plus the air resistance. When the forces are balanced, you will move at a steady speed. When you either get tired and pedal less quickly or ride up a hill, the forces will no longer be balanced and the bicycle will slow down.

Questions

1 Look at the list of words in the box.

  a Which words are 'force' words?
  b Draw pictures to illustrate the 'force' words.

weight	light	friction	electricity
heat	air resistance	twisting	gravity
movement	pushing	height	pulling

2 Your elderly aunt is going in a speedboat for the first time. Write a postcard to explain to her why it is very important that she holds on tight when the boat starts up and slows down.

3 An apple hanging on a tree has balanced forces acting on it. The Earth pulls downwards on the apple and the branch pulls upwards on it with equal force. The apple stays where it is because the forces are balanced.

  a What other forces can you think of which are matched?
  b How can you tell they are matched?
  c Make drawings of examples of balanced forces. Draw arrows to show the directions of the forces.

Unbalanced forces

Unbalanced forces can make moving objects speed up, slow down or change direction. If an object changes speed or direction, then the forces acting on it are unbalanced.

Speeding up

As an apple falls from a tree it speeds up and drops to the ground. The apple falls because the force of gravity is pulling it towards the centre of the Earth. The force of gravity on the falling apple is greater than the air resistance on it, and so the apple speeds up. The forces on it are unbalanced.

Which is greater, the air resistance on the brick or the force of gravity?

Moving on the ground

If something is moving along the ground, a force can also make it go faster. This is called **acceleration**. Imagine you are wearing roller blades for the first time. You need a friend to push you to start you moving. If your friend keeps pushing, you will go faster and faster. The forces on you are unbalanced.

Slowing down

If you are happily moving along on your roller blades and your friend stops pushing, you will soon slow down. The friction of your roller blades on the ground and the air resistance on your body quickly become greater than the forward push of your body. You will soon slow down and stop if you are on level ground.

If you push a toy car across a smooth floor, the force of friction between the floor and the car will slow the car down until it stops. The car slows down because the forces are unbalanced.

Changing direction

In a cricket match, the batsman strikes the ball with his bat. The bat applies a force on the ball, making it change direction.

What would happen if the tree branch was not strong enough to hold you up?

You can also see what happens if something suddenly unbalances forces that were balanced. If a tent has been put up properly, the guy ropes all the way around it are pulled tight. The pull of the ropes on one side of the tent balances the pull of the ropes on the other side of the tent. The two sets of forces are balanced and the tent is ready to camp in. If one of the guy ropes suddenly snaps, the balance of the forces is upset and the tent will collapse!

Why does the cargo on this ship need to be carefully balanced? What would happen if the cargo slipped to one side of the ship?

Questions

1 **a** If you kick a ball across a grass playing field, are the forces on the ball balanced or unbalanced? Why?
   b Which forces make the ball slow down? Discuss this in a small group.

2 Angus is a stupid dog. Whenever Angus goes out for a walk with his owner, Lynne, he starts pulling on his lead. Angus tries to run off. Draw a picture of Angus and Lynne when they are out for a walk. Mark on your picture, with arrows, which way Angus pulls and which way Lynne pulls.

What will happen to Angus and Lynne if the lead breaks? Show this on your picture or write a description.

3 True or False? Copy out the sentences below. If you think a sentence is correct, write 'True' next to it. If you think the sentence is wrong, write 'False' next to it.

   a Weight is a force.
   b An unbalanced force is needed to keep something moving.
   c A balanced force makes something slow down or stop.
   d Mass is measured in newtons.
   e If all forces are balanced, a moving object will keep going.
   f Forces are measured in kilograms.

How does light travel?

Light is a form of energy.

A candle flame, an electric light and a glow-worm are alike in one important way. They produce light. The sun also produces light, and so do the stars we see in the night sky. All these things are light sources and the light coming from them travels at a tremendous speed – about 300 000 km per second. In fact, nothing in the world travels faster than light.

Travelling light

The light from a candle flame, an electric light, a glow-worm and the sun and other light sources is given out in all directions. It travels in straight lines. We draw light **rays** as straight arrows from the light source.

You can learn something about light if you point a torch at the ceiling in a darkened room. The rays of light go up to the ceiling in a straight line. Sometimes you can see rays of light coming in a narrow beam through a gap in the curtains. You can see the straight rays of light as they light up tiny dust particles in the air.

Ben has made a narrow tube of black paper. He is looking at the beam of a small torch through the tube. Ben can see the light of the torch from any direction as long as the tube is straight. If Ben bends the tube he can no longer see the light. This is because light rays always travel in straight lines.

Light and materials

Light rays pass straight through clear glass or plastic, clean water or cling film. We can see clearly through these materials. Materials which allow light to travel through them perfectly are said to be **transparent**.

Some other materials will let light through, but they scatter the light rays. You may be able to see through these materials, but only in a blurred way. Tracing paper and many lampshades are like this. You can see the light coming through a lampshade or tracing paper, but you cannot see through them clearly. We say that these materials are **translucent**. The frosted glass used in some bathroom windows is translucent, as are many curtains.

Many materials will not let any light pass through them. Wood, stone and brick are like this. These materials which will not let light pass through them are said to be **opaque**.

Which object is transparent? Which object is translucent? Which object is opaque?

Shadows

Because light travels in straight lines, if something gets in the way of rays coming from a light source, their path is blocked. Since light cannot travel around the object, a dark area of shadow is left behind it. All materials form shadows because all materials block some light rays, even transparent materials, but opaque objects form the deepest shadows.

Questions

1 How do light rays travel to your eye from a lighted candle? Draw a picture to show what happens. Use arrows to show the light rays coming from the candle to your eye.

2 a In your own words, explain the meaning of the following words:

opaque   transparent   translucent   shadow

b What examples can you think of for each one?

3 In a group, discuss, and then make a list of, the ways in which lights are used to send a message. Make a table with two columns. Write these headings at the top of the columns:

'What the lights are doing' and 'What is the message?'

Fill in the table. You might start with 'Traffic lights showing green'.
a Does your table show up any patterns?
b How many ways can you sort the lights and messages into groups?
c Present your ideas to the class.

How we see things

Light makes it possible for you to see. You can see a lighted candle or some other light source because light comes directly from it to your eyes. Most things do not give off their own light. You can see things only because light that shines on them is bounced back, or **reflected**, into your eyes. When there is no light you cannot see anything.

Eyes

You see with your eyes. The part of the eye which lets in light is the dark circle in the centre. This is called the pupil. Around the pupil is the coloured part of your eye, the iris. Your pupils open wide when you are in a dim place; they close down to a small opening when you are in bright light. It is the iris that controls the opening and closing of the pupil.

Inside your eye

Behind the iris and pupil of each eye is a **lens**. Unlike most lenses, the lens in the eye is soft like jelly. Again, unlike other lenses, this lens can change its shape with the help of the muscles around it so that the rays of light going into the eye all come together in one place. This is called **focusing** the light.

The lens focuses the light to form an image on a sensitive screen at the back of the eye. This screen is the **retina**. Because the rays of light cross over before they reach the retina, the image they form is upside-down. Messages about this upside-down image are carried to the brain by a nerve called the optic nerve. Your brain corrects the image so that you see everything the right way up.

An eye in bright light.

An eye in dim light.

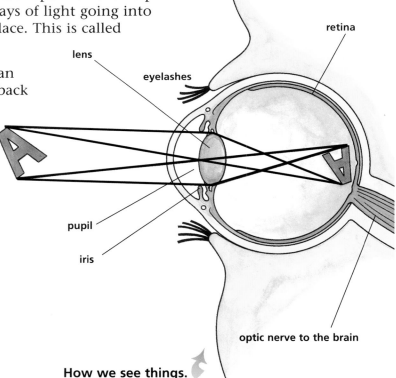

retina
lens
eyelashes
pupil
iris
optic nerve to the brain

How we see things.

Eyes and cameras

Your eye is similar to a camera. Both have a lens, although the lens in the camera is made of hard glass or plastic, not a soft, jelly-like substance. The lens in a camera moves backwards and forwards to focus, whereas the lens in your eye changes shape to focus. The lens in your eye focuses on the retina, but the camera lens forms an image on the film. This image can be developed and printed on paper as a photograph.

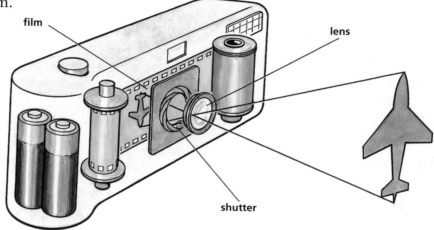

film

lens

shutter

A camera is rather like an eye, but a camera has a film instead of a retina.

Questions

1 Draw a picture of one of your friend's eyes. Colour your picture and label these parts:

　　pupil　iris　eyelid　eyelashes

What does each of these parts do? Write a description next to each label.

2 Can we see the same with one eye as with two? Hold the top of a pen in one hand and the body of the pen in the other. Close one eye. Now quickly try to put the top on the pen at arm's length. Write down what you have learned or explain it to a friend.

3 Look at as many animals' eyes as you can. Handle the animals gently and carefully. Make notes about the following things:

a What shape is the pupil?
b Does the pupil change according to the amount of light?
c Which of the animals needs to see well? Make a class collection of pictures of animals' eyes, including a slug or snail, a woodlouse, a fly, a spider, a snake, a fish, a bird and a cat.
d How many ways can you group the eyes into sets?
e Explain why you have chosen these groups.

Reflections

Light that falls on objects is 'bounced off', or reflected. Everything reflects some light. Although many objects look smooth, if you look at them closely with a hand lens you will see they have rough surfaces. When light rays hit rough surfaces they are scattered in all directions. Some of this reflected light travels to your eyes, which is how you are able to see the things you are looking at.

Still, clean water acts like a mirror and reflects much of the light falling on it.

Mirrors and images

Black surfaces absorb, or 'soak up', most of the light that falls on them, and rough surfaces absorb more light than smooth ones. Transparent objects reflect little light, which is why it is sometimes difficult to see a glass door. If a surface is very smooth and shiny, it acts like a mirror. A true mirror is very smooth and shiny. It reflects most of the light rays falling on it in such a way that you see reflections. You can also see reflections in highly polished metals or paintwork, such as on a new car.

The picture you see reflected in a mirror is called an image. The images in a mirror look clear and life-like, except for one thing: they appear to be the other way around. If you look in a mirror and close your left eye, the image of you in the mirror seems to close its right eye. The image in a mirror also seems to be behind the mirror, not inside the glass.

Mirrors allow us to see things we would not usually see. They allow us to see behind us and around corners.

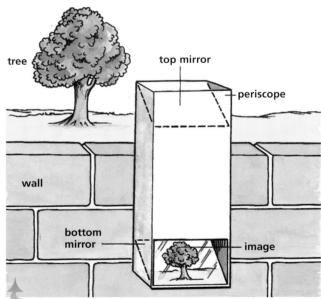

A periscope helps us to see things that are normally out of sight. Periscopes in submarines allow us to see above the water.

Mirrors of different shapes

A plane mirror.

Most of the mirrors you use every day are flat. They are called plane mirrors. Not all mirrors are flat: some are curved. **Concave** mirrors are curved inwards, 'like a cave'. Objects close to concave mirrors seem bigger, or magnified, although you cannot see as much in a concave mirror as you would in a plane mirror of a similar size. Concave mirrors are often used by people for shaving or for putting on make-up. The mirrors used by a dentist to examine your teeth are also concave.

A concave mirror.

Convex mirrors are curved outwards, like a dome. They reflect more objects than a plane mirror, and the objects appear smaller. Convex mirrors are used so that drivers can see behind them. They are used as security mirrors in shops and sometimes by the roadside, where there are 'blind' corners.

More uses of mirrors

A convex mirror.

Some telescopes and cameras have mirrors in them. Lighthouses use mirrors to reflect a bright beam of light to warn shipping of danger. The tiny mirrors in the 'cats' eyes' in the road reflect a vehicle's lights at night and show where the centre of the road is. Torches and headlights have highly polished surfaces that reflect the light from the bulb or lamp. We also use reflective materials on our clothes to keep us safe at night and on the backs of motor vehicles and bicycles to show them up in the dark.

Questions

1 a Which shapes will look exactly the same when seen through a mirror? Design and make some shapes and test your ideas.
  b Write a message to a friend in 'mirror writing'.

2 Make a class collection of shiny objects, which can be used as mirrors. Group the objects according to the different types of images they produce. What have you learned?

3 As a class, discuss these questions:
  a How can reflective clothing keep you safe in the dark?
  b Which people have to wear reflective clothing as part of their job?

What happens when living things die?

All living things eventually die. The reason that the Earth is not covered with the bodies of dead animals and plants is because nature has a way of disposing of dead things – other living things feed on them so that they gradually rot or **decay** away. The organisms that feed on dead plants and animals are often called **decomposers**. Decomposing is another name for rotting or decaying.

Moulds are small fungi, which cause bread and other organic materials to decay away.

Decaying away

Anything that was once alive can decay. Fruit goes brown or mouldy when it is starting to decay. Many deciduous trees lose their leaves in winter. The piles of dead leaves on the ground soon begin to decay away. You can often see the skeletons of last year's leaves left on the floor of a wood, while fallen logs feel soft and crumbly where they are decaying away.

Bacteria and fungi

Small invertebrate animals, such as woodlice, millipedes and earthworms, often break up the dead leaves on the floor of a wood into small pieces. Then **bacteria** and fungi make the dead leaves, and all other materials that were once alive, decay away. Bacteria and fungi are living organisms. All bacteria are so small that you need a powerful microscope to see them. We call these tiny organisms **micro-organisms** or **microbes**. Some fungi, such as mushrooms and toadstools, are quite large but many are very small and you notice them only if lots of them are growing together. The moulds that grow on stale bread and rotting fruits are tiny fungi.

There are many colourful kinds of fungi which are poisonous, although they do help materials to decay away.

A simple, home-made compost bin.

Decomposing

Bacteria and fungi have no mouth, so they cannot eat like an animal. Instead they produce a liquid that slowly dissolves the dead plant or animal they are feeding on. Then they absorb this liquid back into themselves. It can take a long time for a large plant or animal to be decomposed away.

Compost

A compost heap is a way of making use of the bacteria and fungi that decompose waste materials. The best compost is made from soft matter such as grass mowings, dead leaves, tea leaves, straw and vegetable peelings. In dry weather the compost heap needs to be watered regularly, while in winter it can be covered with an old piece of carpet or plastic sheeting to keep it warm. The material decays faster if the heap is turned and mixed up every few weeks.

After a month or two the compost heap becomes a pile of crumbly, dark material. If this compost is dug into the soil, it will form humus, which improves the soil texture. The humus slowly decomposes away to form mineral salts that plants can use as food.

Questions

1 What happens when a tree dies? Draw a storyboard to describe how a tree might fall to the ground and then eventually decay away.

2 Which kinds of tree leaf do you think will decay fastest? Plan an investigation to find out.
   a When will you collect the leaves?
   b What will you do to them to make them decay?
   c What measurements will you take and how will you record your results?
   d How will you make sure that your investigation is fair?

Try out your ideas to see if they work. What did your investigation show?

3 Some waste materials and litter are said to be 'biodegradable'. This means that they can be decayed away by micro-organisms. Other materials, such as plastics, that will not decay away are said to be 'non-biodegradable'.
   a Just by looking, <u>not touching</u>, carry out a survey of the litter people drop in and around your school. Work in a small group.
   b Which of the litter is biodegradable?
   c Which of the litter is non-biodegradable? Make a wall chart to present your results.

Food and decay

The temperature in this freezer is below minus 18°C. At these low temperatures, fungi and bacteria cannot grow.

Bacteria and fungi need food, warmth and moisture if they are to grow. Unlike plants, bacteria and fungi do not need light. If you leave moist foods in a cupboard and forget about them, they will go bad. The tiny spores of bacteria and fungi land on the foods from the air. As they grow, the bacteria and fungi produce chemicals that allow them to dissolve the foods. These chemicals can make us ill. Then we are said to have food poisoning. Fortunately, there are several ways we can stop or slow down the decay of our foods.

Preserving food

Freezing

Bacteria and fungi cannot grow when the temperatures are very low – they need warmth. One way of preserving food until we are ready to eat it is to freeze it. With these low temperatures, bacteria and fungi stop growing. Most types of food can be preserved by freezing, including meat, fish, and some fruit and vegetables. We can also stop fresh food from going bad for a few days by keeping it in the refrigerator.

Drying

In some hot countries, pieces of meat and fish are dried in the sun to preserve them. Bacteria and fungi cannot grow on dry food.

Bacteria and fungi also need moisture if they are to grow. If foods are dried and then stored in a sealed container, the bacteria and fungi cannot grow. Foods that are preserved by drying include some vegetables and fruits, as well as soup, milk and cereals, and pulses such as lentils, chick peas and some beans.

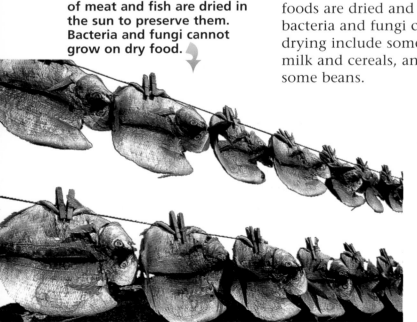

Chemical preservatives

Safe chemicals can be added to food to stop the bacteria and fungi from feeding and growing. A lot of sugar is added to fruit to make jam and marmalade. The sugar stops the bacteria and fungi from feeding and growing. Vinegar, used in pickles, is too acid for bacteria and fungi to be able to grow, while, when bacon is produced, salt is used to preserve it. Bacteria and fungi cannot grow where there is a lot of salt.

Canning and bottling

Some foods are sealed inside cans or jars after they have been heated strongly to destroy any bacteria and fungi. Since no more bacteria or fungi can get into the can or jar, the food will last for many months or even years.

When fruit or vegetables are canned they are cooked to kill any germs and then sealed in airtight containers so that no more bacteria and fungi can get into the food until the can is opened.

Taking care

However our food has been stored or preserved, it is important that we are careful when we handle it. There are bacteria everywhere and some of them are harmful. A bacterium can divide into two new bacteria in minutes if it is kept warm and moist. There are bacteria in our noses and throats and in cuts and sores on our skin. There are bacteria on our hands, particularly if we have been to the lavatory or have touched an animal. Mice, rats and flies can pass bacteria on to the food we eat. The surfaces where we prepare food need to be very clean, or bacteria will spread to the foods we eat and may make us ill.

Always wash your hands after visiting the lavatory and after touching an animal.

Questions

1 In the kitchen it is important to keep food covered, to heat food properly when cooking it, and to store raw meat away from cooked meat. Why are each of these three things important in fighting diseases and illnesses? Discuss this in groups, then present your ideas to the class.

2 a Make a list of all the foods you eat during the next three days. Write the letter D against those that were dried, C against those that were canned, and F against those that were frozen.
  b How would you change your eating habits if the freezing and canning of food had not been invented?

3 Imagine you lived 400 years ago. Do some research, then make an illustrated article for a magazine to answer these questions:
  a How would you have preserved food to make sure your family had enough to eat during the winter?
  b What kinds of foods would you have preserved?
  c What foods that you eat now would not have been available then?

4 Visit your local supermarket. Look around the shelves and list the different ways in which the food has been preserved. Are any foods preserved by more than one method?

Micro-organisms and disease

Bacteria and the smallest fungi are micro-organisms, but the tiniest micro-organisms of all are **viruses**. They are so small that it would take 6 million of one of the smallest viruses to make a row just 1 mm long. The micro-organisms that can make us ill include some bacteria and viruses and a few fungi. The micro-organisms that make us ill are often called **germs**.

Some illnesses that are caused by micro-organisms

Bacteria cause	Food poisoning
	Whooping cough
	Boils
	Some kinds of pneumonia
	Leprosy
	Diphtheria
	Tooth decay
Viruses cause	Colds
	Influenza ('flu)
	Measles
	Mumps
	Chickenpox
Fungi cause	Athlete's foot
	Ringworm

Spreading germs

Sneezing and coughing can spread germs. Dirty skin and hands, and unbrushed teeth, can also cause germs to spread and multiply. Being careless when storing, preserving or handling food can spread germs, while dirty dustbins can attract flies, rats and mice.

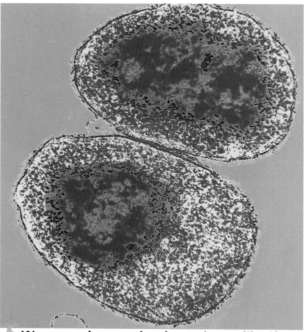

We can only see what bacteria are like if we look at them through a powerful microscope. These bacteria cause meningitis.

We can also catch some kinds of germs by touching a person who already has some kinds of illness. Animals, such as flies, which carry germs on their legs and mouthparts, can leave germs behind when they have been feeding.

Colds

Colds are caused by viruses. If a friend or a member of your family has a bad cold that makes him or her cough or sneeze, some of the viruses will be shot out into the air. If you breathe in some of the viruses, they will settle in your nose and throat where it is warm and moist. There the viruses will multiply rapidly and soon you too will have a cold.

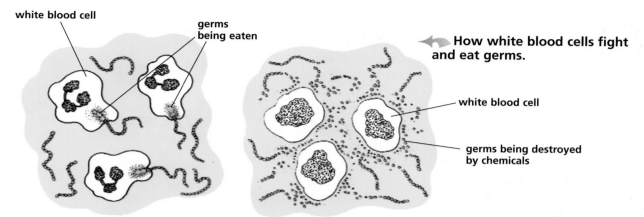

white blood cell

germs being eaten

How white blood cells fight and eat germs.

white blood cell

germs being destroyed by chemicals

Fighting disease

In our blood, as well as the red cells which give the blood its colour, are smaller numbers of white cells. These white blood cells help to protect us from disease. When bacteria get into a cut, for example, the white blood cells move in great numbers towards the cut. They then surround the bacteria and kill them. In doing this, many of the white blood cells die, and their dead bodies form part of the pus which comes out of the infected cut or spot. White blood cells also protect us in another way. Some of them produce chemicals that neutralize, or make harmless, the poisons produced by bacteria.

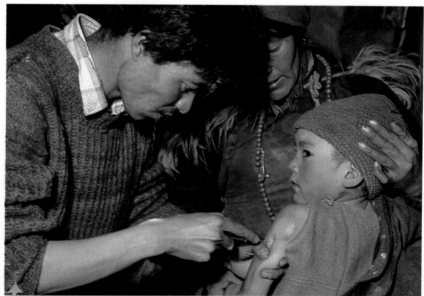

There are some medicines, called vaccines, which help to stop us catching certain diseases. This child in India is being given a vaccination against measles.

Questions

1 Discuss these questions in pairs or groups:

  a Why are people more often ill during the winter than they are during the rest of the year?

  b What kind of illnesses do people often get during the winter?

  c How are these illnesses spread?

2 Why should we keep ourselves clean? Write down all the reasons you can think of.

3 Design and make a poster to encourage people either to wash their hands after going to the lavatory or not to cough and sneeze over other people.

Useful micro-organisms

Many people think that all micro-organisms, such as bacteria and fungi, are harmful. This is not true. We have already seen how bacteria and fungi decompose dead plants and animals so that the materials they are made of can be used by other living things. Without these micro-organisms the countryside would be piled up with dead plants and animals.

Sewage

In a sewage works, waste water is cleaned before it is put into a river or the sea. The waste passes through filter beds containing sand and gravel. These are covered by micro-organisms which feed on the sewage as it passes over them. The micro-organisms break down the waste materials quickly and so help to clean the water.

Bread

Yeast is a tiny fungus that is used in making bread. When they are warm and moist, the tiny yeast cells feed on the sugar which is in the bread dough. In doing so, they make two waste products: carbon dioxide gas and alcohol. The carbon dioxide makes the dough 'rise' so that the bread is packed with little bubbles and has a light texture. The carbon dioxide and alcohol evaporate away when the bread dough is baked.

Beer and wine

Yeasts are also used to make beer and wine. In making beer, a special yeast is added to water, barley, hops and sugar and kept warm. The yeast feeds on the sugar and makes alcohol and carbon dioxide. Wine is made from crushed grapes. In the case of wine, the yeast already grows wild on the skin of the grapes. The yeast feeds on the sugar in the grape juice and produces alcohol, with carbon dioxide as a waste product.

Yeast cells grow rapidly if they have food and moisture but you can only see them with a microscope.

The yeast that turns grape juice into wine grows on the skin of the grapes.

Certain useful bacteria help to turn milk into cheese.

Cheese and yoghurt

Both cheese and yoghurt are made from milk with the help of bacteria, although different kinds of bacteria are used for each. For both yoghurt and cheese the bacteria are allowed to grow and multiply in warm milk. They make part of the milk solid, and also produce chemicals which give the solid part of the milk a particular flavour. Fruit or flavouring may be added to the yoghurt. In a few kinds of cheese, such as Stilton, a fungus or mould is added to the cheese while it is ripening. This harmless fungus makes the cheese look blue and gives it a special flavour.

Other useful micro-organisms

Certain bacteria are also used to make vinegar and some important medicines called antibiotics. Some bacteria are used to extract metals from the rocks in which they are found. The valuable metal uranium can be extracted in this way. Micro-organisms clean the skins of dead animals before they are turned into leather. There is also a useful type of bacterium that feeds on oil. When the oil tanks on ships and in oil refineries need cleaning, these bacteria are used to feed on the waste oil. When all the oil has been decomposed away, the tanks can then be washed out ready for the next load.

Questions

1 a What is an antibiotic?
   b Which scientist discovered antibiotics?
   c What is the name of the antibiotic he discovered?

   Use reference material to find the answers.

2 Go to your local supermarket and find out the names of some famous cheeses.

   a On a map of the world, mark the places where these cheeses are made.

   Look at the wrappers the cheeses are sold in to obtain this information.

   b What kinds of milk are these cheeses made from?
   c Choose one of the cheeses and research how it is made. Make a presentation to the class.

3 Milk is often pasteurized to kill harmful germs. It is heated to 60°C, then cooled quickly. In a small group, find out the answers to these questions:

   a Who invented pasteurization?
   b When is the milk pasteurized? Draw a storyboard to show how it is done.

Reversible changes

Scientists study how to change materials so that they can make new materials. **Reversible changes** do not produce any new substances. They are sometimes called **physical changes**.

You have already met many examples of reversible changes. Changes of state are reversible changes. When you heat water, it turns into a gas, water vapour or steam. If you cool the water vapour or steam, it turns back to liquid water. If you freeze water, it turns to solid ice. If you then warm the ice, it turns back to liquid water.

How is this change reversible?

When candle wax is heated, the solid wax melts and becomes a liquid. If you cool the molten wax, it becomes a solid again.

How is this change reversible?

Insoluble and soluble materials

Insoluble materials can be separated by sieving and filtering. If you cook rice in boiling water, you strain the rice in a sieve to separate it from the water. If you make a cup of coffee using ground coffee beans, you need to filter the mixture. You can put the ground coffee into a filter paper in a special holder and pour hot water over the coffee. The filter paper will allow the water and coffee solution to pass through into the cup, while the insoluble coffee grounds are left in the filter paper.

Dissolved solids can be recovered by evaporation. If, for example, you dissolve some salt in water you make a salt solution. If you heat the solution, the water evaporates away, leaving the salt behind.

How is this change reversible?

Changing shape

There are many kinds of reversible changes where you simply change the shape of a substance. When you cut a piece of wood, metal or paper in half, you change its shape. You do not alter the way the wood, metal or paper is made, though. When you stretch an elastic band, you alter its shape but it is still made of elastic. This is another reversible change

Questions

1 What is a reversible change? Describe it in your own words using examples.

2 List examples of each of the following changes that happen in your home:

   melting   evaporation   freezing   condensation

3 True or False? Copy out the sentences below. If you think the sentence is correct write 'True' next to it. If you think the sentence is wrong write 'False' next to it.

   a All solids dissolve better in cold water than in hot water.
   b Gases cannot dissolve in water.
   c Sugar, salt and instant coffee can all dissolve in water.
   d Water and petrol are solvents.
   e Seawater has salt dissolved in it.
   f Fizzy drinks have oxygen gas dissolved in the liquid.
   g There is no limit as to how much sugar will dissolve in a cup of water.
   h Sugar lumps will dissolve faster than granulated sugar in cold tap water.

Irreversible changes

Irreversible changes start with one material and end up with one or more new ones. In these irreversible or **chemical changes**, the change is permanent. The new material is completely different from the original material.

These changes are very quick, but why are they irreversible?

Cooking food

Cooking food is an irreversible change. A boiled egg or a fried egg looks completely different from a raw egg. You cannot turn a boiled or a fried egg back into a raw one.

Why is this change irreversible?

If you mix together flour, butter, sugar and a little baking powder you get a mixture for making cakes. If you stir in milk or water and cook the mixture, an irreversible change takes place. It is impossible to turn the cake back into the various substances you started with.

Changes caused by living things

Living things can also bring about irreversible changes. We have already seen how yeast, a fungus, is added to moist bread dough and kept in a warm place. The yeast feeds on the sugar in the bread dough, turning it into carbon dioxide gas and alcohol. The carbon dioxide makes the bread rise. When the bread is baked, the carbon dioxide and alcohol are driven off. There is no way you can turn bread back into the dough it was made from, and you cannot collect the carbon dioxide and alcohol to make the sugar you started with. These changes are irreversible.

In a similar way, we have seen how different kinds of bacteria turn milk into cheese or yoghurt. These changes are irreversible.

New materials from mixtures

If you stir a little bicarbonate of soda into vinegar, the mixture fizzes violently. The gas carbon dioxide bubbles off and a new substance is left in the container. Scientists make many new materials by mixing together substances in this way.

If you mix cement powder, sand and water and leave the mixture to stand, it will set hard. A new substance, mortar, is formed. Similarly, if water is added to plaster of Paris powder and the mixture is then allowed to stand, it sets hard. A new substance has been formed.

Why is this change irreversible?

Rusting

The metal iron shows another kind of irreversible change. If you leave a piece of iron outside, before long it turns brown and crumbly. This rust is a completely new substance. You cannot easily turn it back into the iron you started with.

Never invent your own experiments using chemicals.

Questions

1 a What common foods can you think of which change colour when they are cooked?
  b What other ways can you think of in which food changes when it is cooked?

  Make a chart and draw pictures to record your ideas.

2 a Drop some pieces of egg-shell into a jar of water. Look at them after a few days. What do you notice?
  b Now drop some pieces of egg-shell into a little vinegar in a jar. Look at them after a few days. What do you notice?

  Write down what happens.

3 Try out some of the changes described on these pages, but ask an adult to help you. Draw labelled diagrams to show what happens.

Burning and change

Burning is an irreversible process. When a piece of paper burns you see smoke and flames. The flames are hot. You are left with the grey powder we call ash. The ash is a new substance and you cannot turn it back into the paper you started with.

Burning and gases

▲ **In a lighted candle, it is burning gas which produces the flame.**

Whatever you burn, whether it is a liquid like paraffin or a solid like paper or coal, it must first be turned into a gas before it can burn. When you light a candle, you melt the wax on and around the wick. Some of the wax boils and gives off a gas which catches fire. This produces heat which melts more wax, and this boils and gives off more gas which continues burning. Other fires work in a similar way, and all these fires produce irreversible changes.

Oxygen and burning

When substances burn, they use up oxygen gas from the air. They form new chemicals called oxides. Substances cannot burn without oxygen. The burning substance and the oxygen react together in an irreversible change, which produces light and heat. Most things that burn in air need to be heated to a certain temperature before they will burn. Things that will burn in air burn even better in oxygen.

Fuels

A fuel is a material that is used to produce heat and other forms of energy. Most of the world's energy comes from the so-called 'fossil fuels': coal, oil and natural gas. They are called fossil fuels because they are the remains of plants and animals that lived millions of years ago. All these fossil fuels produce flames and gases when they burn. The change is irreversible.

Wood and charcoal

Wood is also a fuel. Like other fuels, when wood burns it combines with oxygen, and smoke and flames are produced. All that is left of the wood after burning is a small quantity of grey ash.

▲ **When wood burns it leaves ash.**

It is also possible to burn wood so that a different irreversible change takes place. If wood is burnt in a special oven so that it gets less oxygen than usual, the wood does not burn completely to leave ash. Instead you see the black substance, charcoal. Charcoal is used mainly for cooking and sometimes for heating, but some is used in making certain metals from their ores. Charcoal is also used for drawing and making paints, paper, inks, rubber, gunpowder and fireworks.

Never invent your own experiments using chemicals, and do not burn any substance unless an adult is present.

A charcoal kiln.

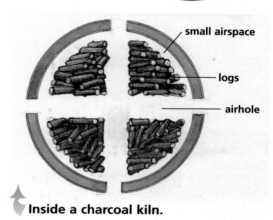

small airspace

logs

airhole

Inside a charcoal kiln.

Questions

1 Think about each of the following changes. For each one say whether the change is reversible or irreversible.

  a Water freezes.
  b Wood and paper burn to ash.
  c Clay is baked into a brick.
  d Puddles evaporate into the air.
  e Natural gas burns to produce heat energy.
  f A piece of iron rusts.
  g A piece of chocolate melts.
  h Someone cooks scrambled eggs.
  i A cow eats grass and later produces milk.

2 Look at the following list of materials:

  paper rock butter sand coal wax ice-cream oil wood

  a Which of the materials will burn if you put it in a flame?
  b Look around your home for objects which have a label warning that they may catch fire easily. You may see the word 'flammable'. Make a list of the objects and record the materials they are made from.

3 Make a list of all the words you can think of which are to do with burning and fire. Flame, smoke, burn, blaze, heat and fire-engine are just a few examples. Write sentences using each of these words.

Glossary

Acceleration The rate at which speed increases.

Air resistance The friction force which slows objects moving through the air.

Amphibians Animals with backbones that live on land and in the water. For example, frogs, toads, newts and salamanders.

Bacteria Tiny living things, some of which are harmful germs, others of which are useful because they help dead materials to decay.

Battery A device that makes and stores electricity. It consists of two or more electric cells joined together.

Birds Birds are two-legged, warm-blooded animals with backbones, feathers, wings and a beak.

Cell A tiny part of a living thing; an electric cell is used to make electricity.

Chemical change Another name for an irreversible change.

Chlorophyll The substance that gives plants their green colour. Chlorophyll helps a plant to make its own food using sunlight.

Circuit The path an electric current takes around a loop of wires and connections.

Classification The ordering of plants and animals into groups. Each group contains organisms that are similar in important ways.

Concave Curved inwards, like a cave.

Conductor A material that allows electricity, heat or sound to pass through it.

Consumer An animal which eats plants or other animals.

Convex Curved outwards, like the back of a saucer.

Decay What happens when dead plants and animals rot away. Decay is caused by bacteria and fungi.

Deciduous Describes a tree which loses its leaves in the autumn and grows new ones the following spring.

Decompose To rot or decay.

Dense Something that is heavy for its size.

Dissolve When a solid or a gas is taken into water, or some other liquid, it dissolves in the liquid and forms a solution.

Evaporate When a liquid changes into a vapour because it has been heated it is said to evaporate.

Evergreen A tree which does not lose all its leaves in one season, but instead loses them a few at a time throughout the year.

Fertile A good soil, which is capable of growing many crops, is said to be fertile.

Fish A large group of cold-blooded animals with backbones that live in water. They have gills to breathe with and fins to help them move or swim.

Focus The point at which light rays meet to form a clear, sharp image after passing through a lens, or being reflected from a mirror.

Food chain A series of living things that depend on each other for food energy. All food chains begin with green plants.

Food web A linked series of food chains.

Force Any kind of push or pull.

Friction The rubbing of one object against another and the resistance felt between them.

Fuel A material that is burned to produce heat or other forms of energy.

Fungus (plural **fungi**) Any one of a large group of simple organisms that includes mushrooms, toadstools, yeasts and moulds.

Fuse A safety device that contains a short piece of thin wire that melts if too much electricity passes through it.

Generator A machine that produces electricity when it is turned.

Germ Another word for micro-organism, especially one causing disease.

Gravity The attractive force, or pull, which acts between all objects. We only notice gravity when one of the objects is very large, such as the Earth.

Habitat The place where a plant or animal lives.

Herbivore An animal that eats plants, especially a mammal. Herbivores' teeth are shaped for grinding plants.

Humus The decayed plant and animal material in the soil.

Hydro-electric power Electricity produced using the energy of moving water.

Insoluble Will not dissolve (become a solution), like sand in water.

Insulator A material which does not let electricity pass through it easily.

Invertebrate An animal without a backbone.

Irreversible change A change that produces new materials that cannot be changed back to how they were originally.

Key A chart or list that enables you to place living things into their correct groups or to identify them.

Lens A transparent object, which focuses light rays and makes an image.

Loam A fertile soil formed from roughly equal amounts of sand and clay mixed with humus.

Mammal A warm-blooded animal with a backbone that produces milk to feed its young.

Mass A measure of how much matter there is in an object. Mass is measured in kilograms.

Micro-organism / Microbe A very small living thing that can be seen only with a microscope. Micro-organisms include bacteria and fungi.

National Grid A system of linked electricity pylons and cables that allows electricity to be sent over the whole country.

Newton The unit of force, named after English scientist, Sir Isaac Newton (1642–1727).

Opaque Describes a material or object that you cannot see through because light does not pass through it.

Organism A living thing.

Parallel circuit A circuit in which the components are connected to each other so that the electric current has a choice of routes.

Photosynthesis The way in which green plants make their own food using sunlight to turn carbon dioxide and water into carbohydrates.

Physical change Another name for a reversible change.

Power station A building or place where electricity is produced.

Predator An animal which eats other animals (also called a carnivore).

Prey The animal hunted by a predator.

Producer A green plant which uses the energy of the sun to make its food so that it can grow and reproduce.

Ray One of the straight paths along which light travels.

Reflection Light bouncing off an object; the 'picture' in a mirror or some other shiny surface.

Reptile A cold-blooded, scaly animal that lays eggs and can live in dry parts of the world, such as a snake, lizard, crocodile, turtle and tortoise.

Resistance The property of some materials that reduces the flow of electricity.

Retina A layer of nerve cells at the back of the eye which detects light and colour and sends information to the brain.

Reversible change A change, such as a change of state, where the materials can be returned to how they were originally. Melting, freezing, evaporating and condensing are reversible changes.

Saturated solution A solution that contains all the dissolved substance it can hold.

Series circuit A circuit in which the components are connected to each other so that an electric current has to flow through all of them before it gets back to the cell or battery.

Solar power The use of energy from the sun to produce heat or electricity.

Soluble Able to be dissolved in a liquid.

Solute The substance dissolved in a liquid to form a solution.

Solution A liquid in which one or more substances are dissolved.

Solvent The liquid part of a solution.

Species One kind of animal or plant.

Spore A special cell with which fungi, ferns, mosses, liverworts, lichens and some bacteria reproduce.

Symbol A sign, letter or diagram that represents or stands for something.

Terminal One of the parts of a battery to which the wires must be connected in a circuit.

Translucent A material that allows light to shine through, although you cannot see through it clearly.

Transparent A material that you can see through perfectly clearly.

Turbine A type of fan which is turned by steam, water pressure or the wind.

Upthrust The force which pushes objects up in water or air.

Vertebrate An animal with a backbone.

Virus A tiny living thing, smaller than a bacterium.

Volt A unit of electrical power named after Alessandro Volta (1745–1827).

Voltage The force of an electric current, measured in volts.

Weight The effect of the pull of gravity on a mass; the measured heaviness of an object. Weight is measured in newtons.

Index